Idolatry of the Translated Forms

Idolatry of the Translated Forms

Fait Muedini

K&B

Published by:

Kennedy & Boyd
An imprint of Zeticula Ltd
Unit 13
196 Rose Street
Edinburgh
EH2 4AT
Scotland
http://www.kennedyandboyd.co.uk

First published in 2020

Cover photograph:
Ceramic Dervish by Aylin Bilgiç
(https://www.aylinbilgic.com/)
courtesy of Fredi Siva at Gallery Iz
(https://www.facebook.com/galleryiz/) © 2020

ISBN 978-1-84921-209-0 paperback

To Kaltrina, Edon, Dua, Atli & Mudzefer Muedini,
and to all those who have understood.

Table of Contents

In the Silk of Oneness

Enemies come at the lovers with sharp arrows, hoping to pierce the armory, hitting tender arteries.

Drag my body through dusty streets if you will: it will only collect the dew of the Divine.
Like condensation from a tea mug on a brisk Tuesday morning, I evaporate into the atmosphere, no longer in previous bodily form.

How many lifetimes did it take me to be me, only to now lose me, thus gaining Everything?

Too many, or too little to count. Maybe some of my atoms were part of previous mystics, whereas others more distant on the spiritual spectrum.

Regardless, I am here now. I have been shot in every chamber of the heart, and cursed with all foul words known in this language.

And yet, the ducks gliding gallantly are My Witnesses; the Ground of God.
I hear footsteps. Be they of enemies, or of my children rushing to provide a profound hug.
I embrace the Everyday; There are no commercials from the Only Program.
God is, and God is.
I wash my hands of the idols of duality
I cleanse my face from the wrinkles of separation.
Lions are tamed by mystics not because of some special power.
What is the point to express fear when hunter and hunted exist no more? In a natural rest the large cats shall reside. In their eyes, God. In their paws, God. In their whiskers, God.

In nowhere and everywhere. Here and not here.
The mountain's base and its peak. Paths and forests.
The lyre is strum by both the beginner and the professional.
Five angels painted with Basquiat, and
Sanai sat to dinner with Huxley and Watts, although each
left their plate full.

The weave of humanity is bundled into the universe
underlying universes, and sewing pins are lost in the silk of
Oneness.

A Jewel in the Crown

Who is asking to feel something in order to believe in God?

That is your bar, and your random demand?

I laugh: in stillness is Everything

You ask for morsels when the oceans are filled with the intoxicating taste of chocolate.

Dream bigger

Why ask for a spot in the courtyard when you can be a jewel in the Crown?

Intoxicated Angels

I resist accepting the narrative that a Journey is required to reach The Beloved

      Any notion of leaving implies the location is less than Holy Blasphemy

The reality is a purging of false images and idols.

Think of the situation as more attune to a housecleaning.

The Beauty is already in the bones, and on the walls. But dust, and boxes filled with the unnecessary block the true Majesty of what lies underneath.

Take time to organize, and more time to minimize.
      Remove all that fogs mirrors
And please, please, don't think for a moment that the grounds outside your abode are more holy than where you lay your head to rest.

Would you open the door to The Divine by saying nothing sacred exists here?

The journey is nonexistent; separation is nonexistent

You are nonexistent; just wipe away ideas desecrating the Purity of Love

And what stands?
      A lover and Beloved dancing gracefully under the pre-fajr moonlight, with intoxicated angels strumming violas on the overlooking hillsides.

Before the Before, After the After

Streams of words all drown in the presence of linguistic-less
oceans

Young lovers dance in unison under star-lit evenings.

Before the before, and after the after

Live there, reside in the holiness of all that eternity offers
Desire not to embark upon train rides that promise
enlightenment in some distant land.
      Dare not disgrace the tender kissing between the
sands and the bottom of your soles
Nails entered into Jesus' feet, and his sacredness was as real
after the blood drained

Shed all contaminations of constructions

Throw out the crutches of language,

Whispering whirlwinds, soft spoken deserts and silent
sentences vocalize with thunderous forces; Bhagavan's quiet
lectures mirror Picasso's blue period
      In both, thou are that

Chuckle at those who wait, and similarly, at those whom
have arrived.
      Both are lost. Guide them without guiding them.
Nothing to witness, no departure.
Burn all artifacts that resembled my name and likeness

Muhammad was not against images, but against images,
since your anything is your idol.
      Dissolve, and in the sugar concentration, a honey like
flavor shall permeate

Travel is the spark for fires and innovation: it provides a ruthless awakening
blindfolding the young prophet, spinning in Sufi circles, and throwing you into new spaces, each more lavish and newer than the other.

Krishnamurti plays patty cake with young observers, Porsches race through turnpikes while proud sunflowers dominate Indiana fields.

I disown "where are you from", "who are you," and "tell me something about yourself."
Answer: Smile, smile, and smile.
God's language, all glassy eyed and majestic.
The universe speaks what the universe speaks. You were the crucifixion and the Night of Ascension.

Long bearded gurus make a bet to shave upon tomorrow's break of dawn,
        which never comes
                despite calls of deceit by novices who see the world as now and "then". Surely, these distinctions are divisions from wholeness. Cutting a pie into pieces makes not multiples.

Blueberries are all harvested together, all sing angelic songs when bitten by the organism of Life.
        There is death, and existence too, both sitting quietly on wooden benches, awaiting nothing, arriving nowhere, wishing not. The first winds of winter bring blankets of snow. Seasoned gurus meditate while in their personified and emulated state of a being creating snow angels.

Children who throw snow balls are godlier than priests and imams whose rules cause blindness, and taint the permeation of The Divine's love.

There is no such thing as "too late" or "too early".
Sunsets exist not, nor do raindrops, at least their translated forms of our creations.

We are not to manifest.
We are not to manifest.
We are not to manifest.

Bells toll without guarding for critique. My love, sit.
In here is God. And here. And here. And here...

Verbal Mandalas: Herein Lies God

The millennia of collected habits prevents the butterfly from
free flight.

Cobwebs signify social construction,
For, the spider, before spinning, sat

The mind is nothing but the enemy of God
Language too is an ally in this war.

Vinyl is from a position of history
     Coltrane
Blue Note
     Melancholy,
          Note (nothing)
Authority asks you to scribble notes in Qurans and Bibles
     Shackled and handcuffed outside the walls of the third
heaven.
Separate in eternity,
     Penthouse floors are for beings who need to exalt
symbolism, correction, and ism
after isms,

Quench, collision,

In the silence, lions and sheiks feed walnuts to hungry
students, watching videos of Shams throwing Rumi's books
in gold encrusted fountains.

You were a God before being born.

The devil's trick was not to convince the world of non-
existence, but rather
to trick you into believing there was a You.

Each time you say I, the ego strings the harp, pronouncing to the planet, your expression of self-desire.

Carving mental idols with "me" and "my" leaves no room for Persian rugs for The God.

Yunus was evolved, dissolved.

A 7-string lyre (ist),
      Resituates the soul of humanity, by removing the stains of "each":

Mystics dance gracefully as the teacher claps two dusty chalk erasers together

Verbal Mandalas; herein lies God.

The Theory of Forms

How dare we trim the branches of the chaotic beauty

With each snip, we are digressing from the Order of God.

Our platonic shapes are only shadows of The Ultimate Being

The Only One "is", and whose form is formless

And because we cannot understand The Reality,

we attempt at carving a shape with the objective of attaining some goal—subconscious attempts of reaching God.

Yet, this act Is Pure Blasphemy.

Assigning partners to God...was this not Muhammad's complaint?

Water and Ice

The water molecules are protesting becoming ice; taking on a so-called "independent form", away from the status of unity.

The crackling of the fridge, aiding and abetting in this process is a reminder of the difficulty of being away from God.

So yes, be upset at the electrician for its role as an accomplice,

　　　　along with any other teacher who tells their pupils to "make an object."

Such language, these lessons of independent formation is the only blasphemy that exists.

Enablers of separation

Cardamom

Break away from Sunday, or "this is a weekday". Hate not
Monday, love not Friday.

The Manuka honey is as sweet when you are "sick" as on
your "birthday".

Guitars dipped in Cardamom and incense stroke rhythmic
chords

Addicts keep the pinky nail long, guitars and computer
experts demand a powerful thumb nail

Demand not the direction of Bitcoin markets,
And yes, the Fusion is as divine as the matted Bugatti.

You too have some biases, small, or fast idols stored inside
your mind.

We pay for concerts not to record, nor to place in our
pockets for a later date. The music that is, is, there, now.
Respect the guitar/God;

The Divinity of Presence.

In Here Lies Truth

Sweet violins in unison with the breathes of my children as they sleep.

I revolt against the mind and all its idols.

Quiet raindrops on San Francisco sidewalks, Tokyo rooftops, Albania's slopes.

A few pockets of iron mountain tea, or racecars turning Speedway corners

In the fabric of nothingness is where the idols are suffocated.

Muhammad took to breaking wooden bones, and others spit rhetoric bombs towards mind-harboring falsities.

Yet, no one walks through the park, in all its splendor, and curses the preacher's con; the small grains of sand sat in Witness and sit in Witness.

This idea of witnessing projects duality. Destroy the witness in order to get away with destroy (ing the ego).

The placement of a wedding ring, the grip of a Corvette steering wheel, or summer ducks caught in winter storms on barely unfrozen ponds,

In here lies Truth.

Meditation on Majesty

As God danced in the center of the nightclub,
I, devotee, enthralled
Enamored

Sat cross legged,
On the floor, against the wall
Next to the loud speaker

And lost myself to the surroundings
Meditation on Majesty

There is no such thing as a separate Atlantic or Pacific Ocean
Duality is blasphemy
Duality is blasphemy
Duality is blasphemy
This conversation is blasphemy
I am blasphemous

~~I am blasphemy~~

Keep asking questions
If you want to meet my ghosts.

Diamonds

Yesterday, my daughter presented me with two "diamonds"
    Not real diamonds mind you, but the appearance—due
to its close proximity--would warrant a second look to the
naked eye.

With both of her little hands out, she asks, what are these?

I respond, they are diamonds. They are very valuable.
    To which she responded, "why are they valuable?"

Hours later, I still struggle with a truthful, accurate answer.

Place value on one rock, and make the remaining quarry
jealous. How can you compliment God's right eye and ignore
the splendor of the left?

Is not the tenth finger as Divine as the first?

Small chatter, or deep insights: Do you drink water from the
bottom of the well, and neglect the top layer? It too arises
from the Springs of Infinity.

Exactly

Where does the breath for all movement come from?

Nowhere

There exists nothing outside the boundlessness of infinity

I want you to camp there

Cleanse your mind of thoughts, and your thoughts of mind.

Drink from the rivers and streams,

And eat from the luscious gardens

The mystery (and ill placed necessity) of prayer

To whom exactly are you pleading? Do you know better than
God?
    Nonsense
Does the right hand beg the left hand to change the course of
action?
    Of course not, you say: both are part of One Mind and
One Body.

Exactly

Fruits and Flowers

Purple majestic skies

No reed flue will cry for me, nor will it celebrate any success

But, instead, it will just play.

The same way trees grow, birds glide, and rain falls.

We are here to witness ourselves.

Expectations are the surest of idols.

                                      Your desires
must weigh less than a soft feather.
        We live in two worlds, here.

A virtual reality of sorts—the stacking of day to day tasks,
done proudly and with care.
        At the same time,
Let us remember the story of the Prince who realized that
indeed the atoms of Infinity carry out on their dance; we
dare not interrupt nor recommend a pattern of movement.

Whenever the sun shines, we accept. Who would ask the
moon to move slightly to the right? Or what fool would
demand an ocean be less salty or less wavy?

You have much to learn still.

Keep pulling weeds.
This way, the ground will be clear, and ready for fruits and
flowers.

I Never Lost Anything

I never lost anything.

While I ate the apple and remembered the juiciness, of it, of life, in the end, as Adam awoke in a new state, I too/we too will release the grip of all that was previously clung to.

Concentration in the eyes of my children when hearing a fantasy-inducing story,

Or of a relief pitcher warming up in the bullpen of Game 7 World Series:

Tell me that either of those are anything but holy.

The implications are everything and nothing, all at the same time.

In Everything and With Everything

I sat listening to the winds, brooks, and cows in the early dawn

I took account of the past lives, the silly anxieties, the insignificant concerns

Today, this morning, I merely observed

I observed the heart, its Majesty and its presence

I wandered outside the mind, into the fields of Nothingness

There I saw God playing with Its Hair, twirling the ends into a lovely loop of Infinity

With each turn, the children laughed as if the winds pushed their backs on the white sanded beach.

And here I was: In Everything and With Everything

In Your Words, Blasphemy

It is not that we have found God, and that you have not.

Rather, it is that we have lost our "selves",

And you have not.

What we are saying is the manifestation of the observation

What you are saying is nothing short of heretical

Nothing is Hidden

Yunus holds puppy-less leashes
  into markets lined with judgement

Put the pot over the stove and cook out impurities

The bubbling? Memories, ideas, symbols

   All, gone.

Prepare a cup and soak tea quietly until the Moment of
Union.

The majesty of the 100th name of God.

Nothing is hidden:

False sages promise sacrilege secrets
  Shed them like the skin off a dangerous python

The remnants? Insignificant waste;

Who would look at the snake's shell and say that that was
the unflinching Reality?

In Eternity, there is no Rebirth;
  Monks can tell you this while sunbathing
     With their feet in shark infested
waters

It Is Here

Am I supposed to be freezing in the middle of summer? And burning during the depths of January?

The moon's rays warm my face, and the sun's bare surface leaves me shivering.

I have lost all sense of direction
Food has become dry, tasteless, and irrelevant

This is what Love does

The Beloved melts crayons until no shapes remain;

Just a beautiful liquid, dispersed outside of form,

Flowing, smoothly, roughly, like the rivers of Tao.

If there is a place at all where I can now say I reside,

                                             It is

~~here~~

Kisses Under the Shimmering Moonlight

In the hall of silence, I sit
    Having lost any sense of separation or attachment

I float in the Sea of Everything.

In these waters is You.

I rinse with the oceans of History, and conduct backstrokes
with the waves of my Beloved

I would be remiss if I didn't say "I love you" after walking out
onto Your Shores.
    However, to say these words implies there is room for
hatred.

I have left all manifestations of duality behind in a former
life.
    Here is what is
The remnants which cannot be described, replicated,
duplicated, fabricated, disintegrated.

There IS, and then, the minds of all others who understand
not.

A wooden log dances together with the sea it kisses under
the shimmering moonlight.

Rusty Mirrors

Despite your beliefs, God has not abandoned you.

That is not possible. Can The Beloved tell one lung to not breathe, all the while favoring the other?

When an audience sees a magic trick displayed, no one actually believes that the magician has moved the object. Rather, we understand the illusion of the eye, a veil over what we can (at the moment) observe.

"Our relationship" with The Majesty is similar in that the universe exists in its entirety. We are always at the Right Hand of God.
    We are the eyelashes to a stunning Face.

Just because a mask is temporarily draped in no way suggests
A separation from the circle compared to Those who have lost themselves.

When a home has dust, we restore the shine by sweeping and waxing floors. Not unlike the artists who reflected the Beloved's creation for the world to see
    we too, clean those rusty mirrors, even if at times it means using harsh chemicals.

My Friends Are Not Rulebreakers, Nor Rebels

My friends are not rulebreakers, nor rebels,

Unless your authoritarianism for religion confines the lovers
into separate quarantine:

Then, and only then, will the fangs come out.

Under the moonlight's guidance, letters to the Beloved are
written
  Feverishly
In matters of the heart: There is no time to waste.

Expressions upon expressions fill notebooks and tablets.

We entered into Your Abode, and never came out alive.

The world deems you a Murderer.

Such is the Truth. You destroyed our "I" in one fell swoop
One glance caused a restless heart to cease

I have become a zombie to the irrelevant

Lecture the neighbors with rules of prayers, ways of sitting,
how to hold (or lower) a gaze...

Ask the newly minted Lover how to act when his affection
walks by on the first day of Spring, or the last day or
Summer? He, too, will forget all learned knowledge.

There is no playbook for the one who is in love, who has
been blinded by a truck when laying eyes upon The Beloved.

A fawn in headlights.
  The laws are not purposely broken; it's just that no
city, state, or country exists any longer.

This is the Pure state of the one who is infatuated with The Infinity.

People dance during weddings to celebrate.
    Some of my friends in fact do this, whereas others, well, all they need is a quiet room, a candle, and a night full of stars. This is what has become of them.

So, tell me again, how many extra rakat do you want them to pray during Isha?
    You do that, and I will be in the corner, whispering sweet poetry into the ear of the Most Beautiful.

If you had an opportunity to be with such Elegance, you too would call the imam and explain that you are out sick.

Beyond Purpose

Needing a purpose is Caesar claiming to be God.

Drums remind me of My Majesty
    Whether in Balkh, Isfihan, Michigan, or Indy,

Who dare attempt to Kill God by walking Hallaj to the
gallows? Scrape one speck of paint from the canvas, but The
Picture still remains.

The young child carries the amulet across the room and into
the hands of the Queen. Another carries the blood of Christ
up to the alter.

From a distance, a hooded peasant, armed with books and a
typewriter, records without recording.

Observation meditation without the dictation;

the King dismissed the scribe, and called for more jokers
and jesters.

Never That

People are shocked to see images of an empty Kaaba during the virus outbreak

as if being there would all of a sudden lead you to recognize Eternity.

The building is but a building;

I would be willing to trade the cube for a yellow petaled flower, and so would you, if there was an understanding that all are equal to one another.

Embarking upon the Hajj cannot be done without turning your back on Home.

Here, too is God. Make your circumventions around the fish filled pond, around violinists at Carnegie Hall, or jazz musicians at The Village Vanguard.

Each exhales God's fragrant filled breath.

I will not be the one to tell the miles of ripe cornfields that their role is of little significance;

Nor shall I utter the words "this does not matter" to any being, conscious or not.

Sculptures of David or Jesus displayed prominently, but what of
flocks of geese?
Or a family of orange striped tigers so graciously walking through a rich wilderness?
Are you telling me, without a lie, that their lives are somehow outside the radius of God's Being?

If that be so, then God is not Infinite.
If that be so, then God is not Eternal
If that be so, then God's Beauty is not Continuous.

For a lover infatuated with their Trusted Beloved,
	They will believe many things, but never that.
Never that.

No Kisses Are Needed

"No Kisses" are needed

In the realm of Infinity every birds' flight holds within it
the expression of Love so majestic, so revealing

> that the angels put down their harps and dance.

With this, my Beloved, is Everything.

In the spaces between hearts, in the lifting of fogs
In the dawn break following a torrential storm,

Is You.

Is You, Is You, Is You

I wander gallantly into the river of Eternity, swallowed
whole by the shallowness of Memory
My identity leaves me,
>   Stranded,
>   Blind and alone on the side of the snow bank.
I acquiesce existence in order to gain Existence.

Forever, I reside

In your arms I melt. Two lovers, sharing a first look that now
bonds them
>   Together
Recorded in the Akashic notebook
Under forever extending skylines

This is the First Step

I structured layer upon layer,
Melody upon melody

Heartbreak upon heartbreak.

One breath

The lyricist has within her a musical voice enough for the
Queen herself to step away from the throne for two more
verses.

Yet, the songbird, in her sacred sounds,
        Resists

Power unto social construction
Music itself has a recent origin.
        Before suffering, before smiling, before thinking.

The first human who sat on the hills of the first mountain,
and looked down, and said nothing,
        That was God on planet earth.
That again *is* God on planet earth
That is God and is planet earth.

Take away all the dust that has settled on the soul
Dry or wet rags will both do the trick.

Grab a woven blanket
And just sit
        in absolute silence,
Let the eyes wander not into past ancestral picture book
memories
Nor into distant lands, multiple futures, multiple heartaches.

All, blasphemy.

Even the eyes, the corridors to the soul, as they say, too, are biased with their own prerogative of how, supposedly, the world operates.

Meanwhile, streams sit idly, and the sun radiates, without any introduction to what is religion, what is truth, what is God.
     And this is a loyal disciple
         who has shed all ego, all futures, all pasts, all possibilities, all yearnings, all glory,
     The body knows not when it turns red, orange, or yellow
     Monk robes too got caught in the fence of biasness and symbolism.
God forbid, God forbid, God forbid.

Drums are as holy when they beat as when they don't. God and non-god cannot both exist.

Listen to lovers' breathe. Tell me the exhale is any less divine than their communal inhale; you dare not.

Children pick dandelions for you to take them to work, asking you to place them safely away for a fear of having someone steal what is so precious and fragile.

Let no one steal what cannot be stolen.

Has your mind wandered into fields of somethingness, be they desires, reflections, or points of curiosity?
     Tainted fruits line the King's table. Everyone but the joker eats.
The novice was told to erase the letters of the alphabet.

This is the first step.

Utterances

White vetiver and Reich's Duet
    A day before the next sunset.

Below hushed flower garden beds,
    Another world vibrates

Well, actually, the energy of this world is not lost, not in
some vacuum:
Rather, radiant, in its own striking light.

Sometimes violins sing, sometimes the human voice cries,
And at other times, princes and the court gallop in dance
While robbers plan their next heist

All of this just occurs.

In fifteen minutes or so, the poet puts down the pen for the
day, or for the hour, or possibly merely a minute
Yet, in that time,
                exactly everything happens

The world has no interest as to whether scholars record its
words, or painters sketch its curves.

The Universe is not here to amuse, as you are not here to
amuse
A Calling? Blasphemy

Quiet wilderness, small sparrows, and four-wheel bicycles to
help prop up a child not yet ready to ride alone.

Just this. Sit and recognize
You were never here, but are always here.

Delete the here. That implies there.

Stop uttering such ungodly words.
Stop uttering ungodly words.
Stop uttering
Stop.

.

Nothing

We were puppets to the master (of our mind).

Now, the strings have finally been detached. The cobwebs of memory and symbolism are swept away in the winds of The Beloved.

I have torn what was sewed into my blazer jacket.
        There is something to be said, and that is that
                there is nothing to be said
for the Lover who treks the world to discover nothing is to discover.

In the garden are the flowers, in Nothingness is Everything

I feel the area around my head and arms, and I am tied to nothing.

I am free; Lost in the forest was my identity; Now I grow like an aged Redwood

The sun glistens gracefully as squirrels chase up the bark.

You, With God, Are God

Enter, Enter!

Do you think it matters whether you came on time, or a bit later than you hoped?

Friends shatter hourglasses, and use the sands for ablutions

Pass the wine cup for those with an inclination for drink

And mugs of coffee for sober dervishes.

We cannot say there has been an arrival

Such blasphemy: Arrival from what? From where? Who controls this realm from which you came, and to which you shall return?

You cannot enter. You cannot enter.

You, with God, are God.

Hallaj counts prayer beads while day laborers construct the Kaaba inside neighboring households

Masterpiece

Rumi and Emre both spoke the Divine language,
    With the Masnavi illuminating God's light with
intricate beams of precision, and dissection of words.

Whereas Emre's one-lined response showed the same Glory
with a Strobe.

Some prefer the flow of Messi, others the functionality of
Ronaldo.

In the end, one brushstroke or 100, all reveal a Dali
Masterpiece.

Leaving Behind Ideas

Underselling and overestimating just how warm the sun's kiss is upon your cheek, the wind's tapping of your shoulder, the dagger-like strike of your Beloved's smile.

A million gazes in frosted glass mirrors

Pilgrims bring offerings from their own coffers, and those of distant families who too failed to respond to the Divine romance within their own hearts:

In your travels to reach God, you only stepped further away. Well, this is not actually the case, as God is carried with You, and You with God.

Even this is not true.

You, God. God, You.

Even this is not true

You/God

Even this is not true.

You/God

Close.

Now leave any remaining ideas to "arrive."

Secret Words

Secret words
Right out in the open

Window dressing filled with empty fruits
Internal refugees rushing to consume.
        Gold that makes them none the richer.

In some silent winter
A cool breeze sways rigid branches
Water freezes under a top layer of grass

Come and remove the warm blanket the nurse wrapped you in,
This, and the mother's first words were all the beginning of
an indoctrination away from freedom.

A million stars without labels are what they are
The first naming rights were another step away from yourself.

Moses asking God his name

In turn, God had to speak in language
        To answer a question that goes beyond language.

The secret is that there is no secret.
Do birds hide their song? Do trees cover their dancing? Mars
and Jupiter are Mars and Jupiter (just please don't call them
Mars and Jupiter).

Beauty is all the cracks and crevices in
        Large sprawling cities
Or in open country.

Say nothing unless you believe not in the God that is The
God.

Did you wonder today without thought?
Or, did you pray to yourself within your own thoughts and
ideas?

Sit still...walk still...dance still....
No need for teachers; in fact
        The opposite: bad educators add something
                And take away nothing,
Whereas the good ones
                    Displace a lifetime of heavy baggage.

Right Here

I saw a learned man carrying a large keg on his back as he walked up a flight of stairs.

"Where are you headed," I inquired?
I worried the weight and stress would surely cause severe pain.

"To Find the Origins of Existence, and the presence of God," he stated.

"Put down the alcohol and rest here," I replied.

Rumi Hugs Shams

Sink so low
Into the arms
Of that whom
Is All Things.
Slouch your shoulders
And just relax
Tomorrow exists not
Same for yesterday
Declare your love
The Beloved smiles
As waves crash
There God is
Open mic night
Children laughing uncontrollably
Or midnight skies
Goosebumps from God
Into the Abyss
Nothingness is Somethingness
I abhor Symbols
And their memories
They never forget
That one time
Or the other
Whirl in Baghdad
Swimming in Lake Erie
Lavender laced sunsets
Help me understand
How "I" formed
Despise this tattoo
An evolutionary regret
I know Reality
Children laughing uncontrollably
Late-night Cabaret
Voice shattering harmony
God is Everywhere
Look inside You
Rumi hugs Shams

The Indoctrination of Language

Roaring fires in luxury mansions

And books stacked upon books

In them, lies something special:

But herein lies all that one needs to know;

Outside of them, outside of words, construction, thought,
sits a more precious pearl
One unidentified,

A gorgeous grain of sand pre-tarnished by deep sea divers
        Who assigned meaning and value?

Souls sign stories of stories and sorrows, apologies after
apologies
For the indoctrination of language

In your vanity lies the ruins of God
the fall of Celestial Rome.

The daily ablutions are not literal
                A suggestion: Instead of water, break mirrors
and use erasers and the delete button, scrubbing any words
from our daily vocabulary;
        For they are distractions
The windshield of the McLaren is clear before the sprint
towards the heavens.

Say your first prayer while in silence and might as well call it
a day when it comes to spirituality.

An electrical fire burns outside of the walls of Getty
        Where, on the inside, lives Sage Rosenberg
Lose words and images in order to Create

Rich Perfumes Fill the Valleys of Heaven

I elevate my daily activities, my "accomplishments" and God laughs;
>The sage when Alexander said he was here to conquer the world.

Even the guitar's strings come back to a place of stillness, silence.
>Piano keys return to nothingness, to The Infinity of Unboundedness.

All circumventions lead back to the point of departure

Every drop of rainfall returns to the clouds that birthed them.

Each single plate returns to The Cupboard, whether we're talking cracked clay saucers after serving the simplest of meals, to gold painted art pieces presenting the most lavish of delicacies.

The mystic's job is to smash all pottery into unrecognized dust.

Like Mary to Jesus, you too will have rich perfumes poured over what once was, and what now is.

Let the fragrance permeate, announcing the Messiah's death and Resurrection as Unified Oneness.

This is why rich perfumes fill the valleys of Heaven.

Until Silence

Tomorrow

Cracks form in concrete
Buildings weaken in the knees
And eventually prostrate
To nothingness

Just like me

Just like me.

Love is the wind
And the bulldozer
To destroy any form
Until

Silence

Perpetual peacefulness
God overseeing
All that was
Created
And all has been
Destroyed

With no observer
Except
The Observer

Unified

Sight and Sight Again

Your holiness energy manifests itself whether you are
singing melodies,
Or placing plates on the outside patio table.

The Divine Spark waves bright colors, flowing majestically,
inexplicitly,

The soon to be widow waits word for her wandering
husband's letter of Love

I fell asleep into the sea dissolved

Uninterrupted, tied essentially to mountainsides, sheep
scattering sharply

Hills covered in green moss all the while

Small bunnies leave footprints through frigid lands.

In every single moment I fell for You, time and time again.
    Sight and sight again

Silly

I cannot stand the incessant bickering over how to curl the toes of the right foot during prayer.

It's as if you have fallen in love with a goddess and can't help but fret about whether to kiss the lips or neck.

Silly indeed: all of this. Everything.

Who debates whether one eats the top or bottom base of a chocolate morsel? The prize is the flavor. God is the sugar in all of your sweets.

Let Baklava trays drip with honey

Only, the masses are too busy arguing over what utensil to best use, quick to shun all divergent opinions.

Silly

No one stopped to debate what to wear before sitting under the Tree of Enlightenment.

The saying "cannot see the forest through the trees" must have been about the world's religions. Counting how many times to touch the book, or in what fashion to enter into "sacredness" as if the step before was less holy.

Either God is Infinite to you, or not. If the latter, then all of this is silly. If not, then a lifetime of rules makes up not for even one Alif of Reality.

Silly

Sufis Sit on the Side and Take Notes

Answer me this one question:

Can you see me in everything? Because, I am in Everything.
      I am the early morning winds, and in the moon's smile
of goodbye

I am the hand that holds your hand, and the nostalgia that
plagues your heart.

I brushed your hair and will be the shroud to cover your
final exterior.

You escaped me not during this late, late, late night,

        nor when I brushed sand within your toes.

The shell you stepped on was Me, so was your first, and final
tears.

I never leave you, since the body is not distinguished from
the Mind.

We shall weave a tapestry fit for a dynastic household,
        Our bread will please the poorest of families.

I sing lullabies to you, and the pen you wrote with was my
utterances in liquid form.

In eternity I sing for you, and you, hoping for a treasure, will
hunt for me.

This is my request: I ask you to quit any sense of chase.
There is no hunt when both the animal, and the hunter
recognize each other as what they—nay—we—all are.

The energetic daughter conducts choreography in a living
room studio
        Sufis sit on the side and take notes.

Testimony of Love

Winds whisper incessantly throughout the night,

Searching franticly for the vessel that makes them truly
come alive

And tonight, it's realized: *"Tat Tvam Asi"*

Revel, revel in the reality that You are The Reality

Adorned with pearls, diamonds, and gold
Trembling with musical vibrations
Cadences that project into the atmosphere

Lyrics come pouring out of your soul,
        Brisk waterways tumble down ancient mountains until
they merge
Into deep crystal blue lakes.

Jesus arose Lazarus with his words

Let your testimony of Love be the same antidote.

The Destructive Duality

God is as present in Mecca as in the moment I wiped tomato sauce off my daughter's hand, after her encounter with pizza and breadsticks.

in both, *Everything*

But delete everything, since, the language implies nothing. The destructive duality.

The Dichotomy of Majesty

Lovestruck

There is nothing to fear, here.

Instead, prepare for a journey online anything you have ever experienced:

Muhammad's flight on Buraq.

The Prophet "Returned" but never returned (the same).

This too shall be you.

Cherries will taste differently, sunsets will seem more real, all the while, the world now presents itself as an illusion.

The dichotomy of Majesty
The dichotomy of Presence
The dichotomy of Nothingness

In everything sings the divine spark
Notes rest throughout, waiting to shine

The concert lays at the feet of the beggar.

The Flag of Infinity

Cry loudly from the mountain tops of Olympus, Baba, or Everest

Or the smaller hillside.

In all peaks and valleys is The Eternal.

Whether it is the crying sire, or the silent sage, the manifestation permeates.

In wandering Dervishes, or in balanced ballerinas

The Essence tells secrets to those who will listen.

Take a seat next to the violin and catch its tears
          The drum beats both before going to war and also to celebrate the terms of peace.

I left my mind years ago, and from that day on, went door to door asking for nothing.
An odd event, you say?

I am as holy when I took steps up to the Gate of Eternity, as I am when I depart.

Melt ideas of distance and separation. Reciting Hu, Om, or the name of the Rosebush are all distractions, illusions, idols of the human eye.

Tearing the garments of luxury are no more humble and holy than donning the brown rags of the supposed seeker.

The garbage man who knows where/and collects the trash has still reached the pinnacle, whether in work attire or a black tuxedo.

The true Sherpa plants the flag of Infinity into its own heart, killing everything, thus allowing the sun to shine over the rocky range.

The Glamour and Holiness

What day is today? Is it The Night of Power?

I reply, "It's Tuesday."

The stars are as sacred now as ever, and ever, as now.

Do we ignore and condemn the Glory of God on "non-holy days"?

Holidays and non-holidays are a duality

Leave the duality

I pity the believer who yearns for the start of Ramadan.
    Do you not see yourself as Divine two days before, and twelve days after Eid?

Gold has the properties of gold whether in the form of jewelry or hidden away in a safe deposit box.

The words of The Beloved are written across the skies for all to see,

During the sacredness of yesterday,

As well as during the glamour and holiness of tomorrow.

The Halls of the Beloved

I entered into an open room, with modern garb, and a
learned mind, filled both with positive lessons of how the
universe worked, but also libraries of symbols and illusions.

Like a bear's paw covered with thorns, much of what was
there was important—and necessary—but the intruders
needed to be removed.

What do you think ablutions are for? See the water as an
allegory to what lies behind: the veiling of lessons for those
who understand

In meditation, the extraction of all that is no longer:
    The temporary is flushed into the sea of irrelevance.

Sit quietly and wait for the Guest to bestow Grace.

Like a child holding a mirror for the groom on His Wedding Day,
In the reflection is both everything, but also the illusion of
nothing.

Tao drums, a heartbeat, or 808 machines
Each, a cadence into the halls of The Beloved

The Melting of Relics

A religious pilgrimage to Mecca, The Vatican,
Tiruvannamalai, or Tiger Stadium
        The disservice to God's long robe scattered throughout
the universe

What to make of the tiles upon leaving holy buildings? What
do we call those?

Are the beggars outside the door in some way less than
the gold crosses inside? Both will succumb to the passage
of time, whether naturally in the case of our brethren, or
eventually through the melting of relics, not dissimilar to
their fates during the Siege of Constantinople.

Our time, all time, will eventually come.

        except of course she who subscribes not to the theory
of this normality.

Enter into Everything by emptying everything.

The spiritual bulls come out only after the bears look to have
defeated all who stand.

In the depths of the Earth are where the precious metals
lie. In dusty library corridors are also the Secrets of the
Universe.

The Picture Behind the Veil

You spent a lifetime gazing upon the Earth looking for any wine that will get you drunk.

How, after all the while, did you fail to realize that the flames of Love were kindling the very same fire within your home on those cold Winter nights?

"I need to see this, I need to see that," uttered one who was truly lost.

The Sufis drew a circle and sat;
    The white chalk outlines a dead body.

The rebirth is whatever comes next.

Share meals with strangers and they shall turn to brothers.
    We awake and then can see nothing.
It is only after practice that God's image comes clear in the now perceived objects.

Dust any scene and the fingerprints of God will surely be found everywhere.

Notice and cherish the cuisines of home before embarking onto distant journeys

The moon smiles to both the King and the beggar.
    Whether purple or brown robes
He who is beyond distinction of color has the ability to see the Picture behind the veil

The Sun Sets Equally in the Evening

Stroll through the countryside,

Witness the sun poking its head out, breaking the surface of the horizon

And, instead of judging the way the star shines, just be in awe.

We question not the break-dancer for their abstract expressionism: one line is no more valuable than any (or all) others.

This too is our attitude. So, soak the rays of our celestial neighbor; bask in its glow, its glory, its energy.

There shall be a day when this too fades.
    Cry not, but accept that all except The All has an appointed movement and time.

Do not hang onto that which is not meant to be captured:

    Possession is but a disease of the mind
Trueness is flow
    That is all
Limit reality not
    The mind plays tricks by planting expectations
Stand beyond
What do you call this, then?

Well, nothing.

The sun sets equally in the evening.

The Thorn and the Rose

I came into this evening with a bit of a setback:
    Stepping on the Rug of Evanescence, I realized with me
was a suitcase
Filled with problems of the mind.

Anger is a silly emotion, created by the internal to distance
you from The External.

    Whirling dervishes spin in consistent planetary form
because no thought exists.

Try thinking about each step, and quickly shall the
wandered become paralyzed with inaction.

Remember that each thorn comes from the stem of The Rose

The gambler understands that with the acceptance of Heads
also comes the possibility of Tails.

Iblis was condemned for elevating his own mind and form in
attempts to break from The Formless.

Like Jesus washing the feet of the disciples

I rub dirt on the forefoot, the soles, as well as my Achilles
tendon, recognizing that one cannot understand dirt
without its counterpart, cleanliness.

The Throne of Expansiveness

Your heart, until yesterday, teetered on the unimaginable.

Self-delusion and false grandeur,

They shall be a pain in your side for years to come.

Peel layers of the onion to reach the heart of Reality

Who you were yesterday and who you are today are two
different truths, until you realize they are not.

Sit silently, and, like a sweet spoon in Eternal Tea, dissolve.

We know the saying: Sugar cannot be extracted once mixed

There you are:

Next to Seraphim, sit by the Throne of Expansiveness, and
collect the Fragrance of Everything

Ezekiel waits for G-d's Chariot

An Unnecessary Journey

The novice, first time lover calls out for you, searching for you, digging tirelessly for diamonds and gold nuggets.

The same soul feels slighted and frustrated when they turn up an entire house in search for a lost ring, only to come up with 'nothing'

I laugh from a mountaintop, I smile from the office chair, I shake my head from a distance.

Where to, my child? I ask. Stop: before you answer, know that any answer that involves any location--, and, while not wrong, is just an unnecessary journey.

Why travel to Egypt when the Sphinx head stands tall right in your own backyard?

The river Ganges wishes it could perform ablutions in Your presence.

Worries Amplify Your Blasphemy

Worries amplify your blasphemy

Take the mind: a quiet, somber chamber where either
beautiful music, or just loud noise can echo off its walls.

Each concern is the devil saying, "you are mine."

Shake shackless off
    It takes but one emergency for the "believer" to quickly
dismiss the Divine.
And then what?

Mystics teach the King that "This too shall pass"
    Bow not to the idols
        as they are transported on the dusty road to the
Kaaba
Thoughts, like crass caravans of simulacrum
        are all to be torched with the fuel of hell
      themselves; flames embark on flames, causing
      destruction upon destruction.

Brush fires need to burn forests to prevent larger outbreaks
later on.

The aftermath will be a blank canvas upon which, in time,
sap filled tree bark shall grow, providing sweet nourishment
to all who wonder its lands.

The Promises of the Elsewhere

A pair of birds flew right through the Eiffel tower in excitement of landing in Paris, when the lights were on and everything.

Anticipation of the promises of God, of pastries, of fine breads and dinners.

High fashion, and tourists/idolaters who have abandoned the sacredness of God's kiss.

You visited elsewhere, and all the while turned your back on the holy endeavor?

Stars point not to one another saying, "there, there is the real God." Dismiss a mother's cooking for a downtown feast and see her reaction.

Ask the prisoner how that homemade meal tastes now.

Be here, ever-present, in the living room of The Divine. Your aura, the only companionship.

Quaint picnics on country backroads shall too serve witness to Majesty of Everything.

After Witnessing God in the expansive plains of the Midwest touted lands,
    the promises of elsewhere,
        while equally holy,
        can keep whatever attractions they blind the
world with.

Trumpets Triumph

Israfil's call will not be the end of the world, but a re-awakening of it, where all that was programmed will be lost

Bright mandalas swept away into nothingness and yet, everythingness

To Find Truth, the painting and images have no choice but to dissolve.

The ego is trapped in the pictures.

The Heartbeat of Love

Nationalism clouds judgment.

Man-made roadblocks preventing true union.

Such distinctions are clearly the first form of idolatry and blasphemy

For they not only separate man from one another, but they also divide humans from God.

God said the He created different peoples so that "they may know one another." But often times, they are too busy knowing only themselves.

Their arrogance and pride lead to fighting and disharmony.

The true scholar, the lover, doesn't care about language

And flags are meaningless.

The only space worth occupying, and the only language worth speaking

It the heartbeat of pure love.

The Moon Sat Upright

The blasphemy of tourism neglecting the God that resides in their own homeland.

Sending letters exists only under the condition of being separated from love, from majesty, from eternity.
    A longing to return.

Your wheels need not make a singular circumvention

The Kaaba, or your own home town, equally absolve you of all sins.

Snapping photos of "exotic" elements does a disservice to the loyal soil, who gave itself as a sacrifice to The Beloved,

Dressed in wonderous silks,

Awaiting a mere smile.

You have in your hands the gemstones of infinity.

Look for whom, when God sits in your castle and buys apples from the local fruit stand.

Surely, they know not.

The father, mother, and two children recited pop culture lyrics in a black sedan, all the while eating individually wrapped chocolate bars

In the background, the moon sat upright, beaming.

I, Ishmael

I, Ishmael, place my own neck on the altar

The Angel of YHWH saving me only condemned me...

Recognized,
and thus, not dissolved

Into

                                       That

Dervish

I was tested repeatedly,
My arms thrown about wildly,
During the spring winds and rains.

Summertime, I was berated with shouts of sunlight
    Attempting to withstand hours of heat and humidity.

In the fall, left within nothing
    I stood exposed. I was vulnerable.
My ego emptied
    In front of the world to see.

Yet, I withstood.

Then, in the winter, finally, under the jealous moon,
    I sat still, a dervish frozen,

                           Held silently
    In the arms of the Beloved.

Stones of Illusion

I would write memories of you in stone

But in reciting your name,

I create idols.

I create idols.

In reflecting on memories

I create idols.

Meditation is the Muslims
Who
      Upon conquering Mecca
Went into the Kaaba

And smashed stones of illusion

I smell red rose petals
But ask for forgiveness
For calling them
Red rose petals:

I meant to say: God

I meant to say God:

~~I meant to say~~ God.

~~I meant to say~~
[God]

I curse my tongue for speaking a name
I curse my eyes for creating ideas of images

I wallow in nothingness

Tomorrow, today, young lovers strolling
Into fields of wheat, sunflowers, and heartache
and happiness
    and every emotion in between
There is no "in between"
There is no "is" the way we define "is"
Other than IS (unexplained)
That IS

~~Wander~~

Wander into the forest of non-being
Wander into no forest of non being
Wander not
~~Wander~~

God

I Saw God Today

I saw God today.

We all did, actually.

Whether my daughter, in my arms
Each flying about like she is Spiderwoman

Or yours, playing how they play

Or the tree,
Or the wind,

Or You, in the mirror, losing yourself
And within it, gaining the universe
Beating time by entering into the Boundless.

Whatever sensory experience was it,
Just smile
and remember, everyone and everything
is a ray of light from the Beloved.

Songbirds

Songbirds,

Two, lovely colored
A mirror facing a mirror

...Beyond both

Vibrations, small strings

    Violins play in unison
A concert of Divine beauty

Manifest in concert halls
    And in

A need for Union.
Crave for the world to turn its back onto you
Walk alone on streets that have seen much more, and
remember much less.

I (...)
I (...)
I (...)

I

In a Bed of Fragrant Petals

I regret that I have to utter words
From a language I wish not to speak.

Yes, I am versed in both worlds,
But my heart belongs to my Origin tongue.

Any sense of "I" leads to feelings of condemnation.

The candle's final breath is its most beautiful;
    Feel the edges of the glass:
Question whether the energy no longer exists.

Two lovers cried at the thought of separation
Until the selves were lost
               In death, both lived forever
in a bed of fragrant petals.

    The dervish sits on the bench and observes bees
whispering divine secrets to the stamen. With one word,
everything was born.

Nor the Map

Read the poetry
But upon awakening
Dismiss everything

An explorer
Arriving in new lands
Has no more need
For a boat,
Nor the map

Somewhere

Somewhere,
Sometime ago,
A hidden mystic scribbled
Sweet secrets into the soft clay

Today, they are as real as the most preserved papaya leaves.

The latter, present for billions to read
The former, available for the few to understand.

Shams of Tabriz understood
that like a carrier pigeon delivering valuable
correspondence
the words, at some point in time,
will reach where they must go,
Even if it does indeed take

the entire thousand years

I Write the Pages

I write the pages...

And ask you to

Tear them out

Don't save them: they are of no value in the binding

Use them only to start your fire

Singers Rejoice

Singers rejoice that their voice carries utterances of divinity

The writer makes the same claim for her words

The painter captures love in every stroke

The cook's recipe contains love ingredients, and then shares her secrets with divine fire

The term 'well done' does not exist to this love.

Annihilation is the best compliment to the Chef.

The Years Are Merely Days For Love

The years are merely days for love

This is the true calendar

Measure history based on such events

Remove ce or bce

Begin with the First Kiss

To Eve and Adam, Jesus, Muhammad, Rumi, so on

Let our months be named after characteristics of love, our new year a remembrance that concentrates energies on a unity of days and beings.

Our spring, a time to revitalize passion

Our birth, the fatal separation,

And of course, as Mawlana uttered, our death

The Wedding.

And in between, let time be used only as a means to organize 'love encounters'

Rain Only Exists Because

Rain only exists

Because the cloud had to momentarily turn its back

To let the drops become free
      in order for the longing process to begin.

You don't know God without

First

Not knowing God.

But if you understand photosynthesis

You know that the Lover always

Re-unites with the Beloved.

One might call their relationship

Love/Hate

But it's much deeper than that.

One might be better served to title it:

Longing/Uniting

I think this should also be the label we place on human relationships

Since lovers always find one another.

      By realizing there were in each other's embrace the entire time.

Bodhisattva

I am giving up the present so that you may break away from the past

Bodhisattvas will adopt language to speak with s/he who is still bound to the attachment of conversation.

Do you believe for one instant they want to be adorned with heavy jewelry when the wind's kiss is enough to provide them with joy forever?

Wish not for immediate sleep, nor long, grueling nights.

This is the Fate of Idols

Sparrows,
Somewhere,
Whether singing,
Or sleeping

Both hold mirrors in their left hands,
While sitting next to the right hand of God.
      Scratch that.
They are the right hand of God.
      The red cardinal
Sat outside the Cardinal's office
      Asking him drop all social narrative, construction,
tradition.
The child, sound asleep, speaks her own wordless language
      Smiles while holding striped sticks of bubble gum
Pulling up pink rain boots on a sunny September day.

This is what is
Leave the dictionary in some dingy basement

This is the fate of idols.
      Wandering with God requires saying goodbye to
human words.
Monks wear robes, and bankers wear suits: both are
signaling something.
Rid yourself of something; all things.
      Rest on the broken tree trunk near vacated forests
Have you ever tried to give undivided attention with
thoughts playing like movie reels?
      Blasphemy. Give nourishment only by emptying cloudy
rainwater from an overfilled glass.
Become silent; a redaction of blasphemous teachings. Day
after day, year after year, the devil has carved within the
world statues to be worshipped.
      They take the form of, well, forms.
Ice cream melts whether it is called ice cream or not.

Remember this and understand that the mystic
    Need not stay in one location,
And need not say hello
    Especially with words.
Hello implies goodbye.
    Move away from the well that provides so that you can
also move to the place that is without provisions.
    Some dimension, somewhere? No, this dimension, now.
This is love.

Idols Taint the Now

There is nothing to know
Love destroys all words
And all music.

Stop defaming that what we call "Love."
End the disrespect with language

Wade into the water, under the rising sun,
Or the proud moon...

Remove ideas from the sanctuary
Idols taint the Now.

That's More Like It

The rose bud is ready to raise her neck to the surface of sight
    Any moment now.

Revisionists reinvent received responses
            None of these matters: who sees the sun is who
sees the sun
But remove all of the veils of knowledge, evolution, and
societal constructs
        Here, in this pond, lies flat the lily pad that is God.

Bewilderment, sweet, sweet wonderment
        With this star, or the infinite universe that the eye and
mind, after a point, only trusts exists

Stroll across the courtyard, and watch the fourteen birds
pecking for seeds in the middle of winter, plus or minus one day.

Tomorrow is a construction built by those who had instructors
by those others, who, in their united front, each of which
understood not, that what was, is, only, and nothing else,...

So, today, dance. Child on your shoulders, four quick steps to
the left, and four more then to the right.

Synchronize nothing, misalign nothing either.

                Basho walks up high hills
                Crisp leaves sit on grassy fields
                Rest on old tree stumps.
Something like this?
                Sure.
Nightingales or small robins all have their place
        "their place?" this implies separation.
Let's try this again:
        Nightingales, small robins, planetary beings, stardust, God.

That's more like it.

I Held a Dandelion in my Left Hand

I held a dandelion in my left hand
And a purple tulip in my right.

Until I realized
There was no dandelion
      And no tulip
And no
      Me

~~I held a dandelion in my left hand~~
~~And a purple tulip in my right~~

~~Across from me~~
A Buddhist teacher chopped wood.

God in the Heartbreak

God in the heartbreak
    In the returnless calls
The void of not answering...a ring that enters into *Ein Sof.*

In the sidewalk cracks
Not unlike cracks on an aged smile
    All of the contours
And crevices
    There resides God
There is God
This is God.
This is You.

Campfire

The Advaita Vedanta monk
Picks flowers,
tosses wooden prayer beads into his pocket

and gathers firewood
in solace and solitude

Elsewhere,
Children sit on skateboards
     Rolling
         Down
            steep driveways

"Call Out My Name"
in your own mirror

Sit near pond banks
And reflect on the reflection
Manifest as a Manifested
         Station
         Of Unity.
Be like Ruzbihan and Dance with God
in the early dawn hours

Coalesce around a campfire
Built within the wood of your self
And burn
     All...

Be Light
Be ~~(light)~~
~~Be~~

I Heard a Butterfly Sing

I heard a butterfly sing
And a tree branch dance

Quite simply

I joined them

Only to realize

That sitting,
I too was already connected

God (You)

I see God in you
In the way you carry hard to understand books,
In brushstrokes on an oversized canvas

In the sorrows you have imprinted on your skin
I hear drumbeats and compliment the space between the
thumps
      Kabbalah dreams spread through sun sparkled eyes
I judge not your failures
Rather, only record the expressions of your highest
accomplishments
Even if, for you, is to come to a dinner with a loaf of day-
old bread and a note with a few scribbles of thanks, and a
memory of embracing your beloved on a distant beach
      On a distant memory, in this universe

God sits and dines with mortals
God sits and dines with Itself
God sits
You sit and dine
The world observes you, you observe the world
And you both laugh uncontrollably when the makeup artist
pulls out a mirror and shows that this way of language
(understanding) is nothing but a disguise
And that this is this, and nothing more,
      But, nothing less.

Cocoon Glass Cages

The saying "I am not of this world" is true, but false at the same time.

Understand it this way: A voice at the bottom of the mountain will not sound the same as when on its peak. Look at this, that way, too.

The dervish sits in solitude, in physical, and mental.

Yet, there is no physical, no mental, no sitting, no dervish. Prerequisite memories escape cocoon glass cages.

Roses

Roses get jealous when you think about other roses

Trust your memory with nothing; take any keys from this
previous relationship
And change your phone number; there is no reason to
maintain contact with yesterday.
　　　　At the same time, don't make the mistake of inviting
tomorrow
For tea and lunch; the cost will be enormous.

I love the last moments of a song where the border between
what was, and silence, is closest. That last sound is what is
most fascinating.

A veiled smile
Underscores hidden realities
Sing, sing, sing in the garden of lovers
Whether that is in a field of lilacs, a rugged jungle
Or downtown's paved veins.

We see you—here
You are you—here
There is no here

Quiet contemplation
Sure manifestation
Unified congregation
Rewards, elation.

---Kill thoughts (idols)---

Hi, God. Hi, God. Hi, God, whispered, yelled, thought the
Dervish
as he rode his bike from one block to the next.

Sidewalk cracks, building cracks, skin cracks
Piles of sand mounted on top of the others who succumbed
to a similar fate
Fight not.
Ask not for tomorrow, an idol planted the no other than
Satan himself.

Here you are, so hello.

All my words will merely serve as distractions from what
you can already see.
        Please, stop.

See by seeing that there is nothing to see. See?

Yesterday's flower petals released sweet fragrance
She too emitted radiant laughter

And the perfumer captured them both

There is No Life, and There is No Death

There is no life, and there is no death.

I am going to pick flowers, and observe my children's laughter, with absolutely no idolatrous distractions.

Qaf and Jabal al-Nour

> The two gaps in my son's teeth are just as holy as the
> mountains of Qaf and Jabal al-Nour

Your individual consciousness
is the sound that breaks the barrier of silence,

the idol whose image keeps you

from the expansiveness of

                                        God

If I Must Use Words

If I must use words, I shall use them to curse them.

They serve me no purpose—a second kidney in a mind
evolved from needing the function of the body.

Hit your notes when singing
I shall see what is beyond the sheet music.

The recognition of my beginning and my end is an afront to
your
                              Unboundedness.

To bow to time is to build an altar within the body of The
Divine.
Planting a tree inside the depths of the forest negatives the
individuality of the tree—the roots, the bark, the leaves
                    All extensions of what never came before,
and what never dies.

Beyond Graveyards and Gardens

Releasing tears for a death
    while understandable,
Illustrates that shackles and handcuffs
Are solid cast, and iron clad tight.

Clip not the wings of a butterfly with sharp scissors

Sugar dissolves in water for the sweetest of drinks.

The Vastness neither entered nor left

The lovers rolled through the summer's sunflowers,
And long after the footprints on the arduous winter roads
Disappear.

To suggest presence implies absence.

God forbid. God forbid. God forbid.

A never-ending stillness
    Before the wedding
    After the honeymoon.

Not here. Not there.
A red rose holds its head high in Spring
And retreats gracefully many months later.

Petals upon tombstones

Icons distracting from A Majesty beyond graveyards and
gardens.

Infinity Means Infinity

The Apple doesn't fall from the tree
Can also be understood to mean that
    The fingerprints of God are still God
We have an inseparability to us

1000 puzzle pieces all find their place in the landscape of
The Whole

No one would hold up and show off one singular part
without connecting it to its entirety.

Different forms, pictures, and colors? All are beautiful, and
yet, in separateness, a vacuum

Everyone is only happy when The Picture is whole
    How can you minimize your (w)holiness?

What good is a trillion-piece puzzle if even one piece is
missing?

Infinity means Infinity,
Entirety, Entirety.

Tell Me Again?

My Splendor transcends that of even Buraq
For even he took trips back and forth from Divinity whereas
The Master of The Household has not once asked me to
place my shoes back on and retreat from His Abode.

The Pilgrimage to Mecca suggests the Kaaba sits not in the
center of my heart.

My blood performs the circling,
And my tears of joy are the water that springs up from the
well of Zamzam.

Tell me again where to journey
when the destination is none other
than where already rest for the evening, and awake in the
morning?

Footsteps

So, the non-believer sees not the radiance of your
smile?
>Smile anyways

So, the world recognizes not your brightness?
>Shine anyways

So, you doubt your value to humanity?
>Be anyways

Every lavender plant is beautiful in the eyes of bees.

All footsteps are taken on the Body of God.

The Fall

How pretentious to show off your faith through jewelry,
headgear, or a long robe.

Do you think God disavowed the baseball cap?
Just once I would like to see an imam in a backwards fitted.

Tell me to my face that this would be unholy, separate from
The Unity.

Your perceptions and misconceptions are exactly what Iblis
thrives on

The Devil wouldn't exist had we not granted the recognition
      We are the guilty party who planted the seed of its
creation.

God looked away from Adam for succumbing to the false
notion that Iblis was real
      That was the punishment in the story;
The talking snake was but an illusion

Allah never punished Adam and Eve
Instead, they created their own veil by even entertaining the
idea that anything other than Oneness could be.

This was their "fatal sin" that most of humanity still wrestles
with today.

That Which is Perfect

You are not merely atoms or particles
    Such a reduction of God!

Taste the moisture and richness of flaky croissants

    Is that not perfection?

Yet, no one would dare diminish a single grain of powdered
sugar
Each ingredient,
    Every fold upon fold
    Layers of

        That Which Is Perfect

Adhan

The clerics lecture the community on whatever has
corrupted their fickle minds;

Their dogma, interrupted by the call to Prayer.

You need the adhan to remind you of God?

Were the budding flowers dancing for no audience?

Did not the sun's rays soak into your skin, as you watched
your son build sandcastles on the beach of Lake Prespa?

Seamstresses sew silk saris, all the while,

The Quran calls for witnessing....

This along could be the shortest holy text ever needed.

Each note from the Imam's breath, a reminder that the focus
is away from The Source.

Light flashing, images passing, a daughter throwing karate
kicks, and a son calculating math problems. Keep the adhan,
for the Kaaba's music plays perpetually in my ears, and the
lights of Muhammad's cave penetrate directly into my sight
line.

God Expects Nothing of You

God expects nothing of you

The mountains enjoy sitting idly, offering only their warmth, whereas the goats receive nourishment and shade. And the relationship is one without question.

As the shepherd speaks to God with imagery of sheep, the language is returned, as is the Love.

Renounce not your being.
     Fret not if the slippers are not up to the occasion, or the dress is viewed as less than high society.

No peering eyes are watching; the only gaze is between the Lover and Beloved, and, as two souls madly falling for one another.

The outside world, to those whose hearts pound quickly, does not exist.

Gold and Silver Hidden in the Sparkle of Your Eyes

Straw towers filled with lovers rolling around on the same Earth where Omar Khayyam spilled red wine.

I have witnessed myself, travelled through the world's many paths, finally losing myself, and in this, have found God.

Gold and silver hidden in the sparkle of your eyes.

I Shall Speak Your Language

I shall speak your language,

What language? These words, this language,
    Any language

In recitations of love, my gift comes prepackaged for all to
understand.
Then, a wandering mystic shall revert back home, under the
tent of Oneness, where sound and not sound fight amongst
one another for attention, when in reality, the Parent loves
both
    as all is precious in the eyes of The Timeless.

So, I utter and speak words dipped in sweet honey biscuits,
rich chocolate shells, wrapped in memories you construct
with your future self.

Did you sing into the wind today? With fervor? With
romance?
No other lyrics suffice.

Slide your feet into soft sandals, supple shoes, or enter the
place that needs no entrance with bare feet, open toes,
exposed souls, and an exposed soul.

Your own thoughts shelter you from the rain that provides
nourishment to a luscious garden.

Quit thinking, open the heart to Love, and dance aimlessly
with the universe, for the songs never cease.

Observe the passion of existence; your thoughts are indeed
your idols.
Smash them by not succumbing to the you as god.
You hold no such authority,
    no such status,
        no such power.

In this is the illumination of pure freedom.

Take your upper level undergraduate courses on life, and then, when ready for graduate work, and your dissertation, the learning to unlearn, come see not me, not books, not talks, not...

Numb

Numb to all voices inside and out
                    In parks,
I silence myself
            On demand: three words then to say nothing
Read Mary Oliver during northern winters.

Chemistry utters lovely sonnets without saying a spoken
word.

Have you thought how different "you" would be?
Had you turned instead of drove straight? Applied to a
few more colleges? Reached the stop lights a few seconds
earlier?

Just like that...evidence of being and non-being.

December snowflakes and a family of drakes who were
probably caught up north
Unexpectedly.

        At least for this time of year.

                    Today
                Will be tomorrow
                In someone's mind,
                    Memory

Can you be both hungry and full at the same time?

Say hello to yourself, in fifteen years, after a reformation
within your very being? Quit complaining, stop wishing,
and walk with the thunder of Zeus, and the beauty of all
goddesses in all cultures in all history. And, just like that, you
too become that.

A thousand lines, a few words.

Trade Copenhagen for Detroit...none of this, all of this,
	Sing lullabies, or sit without thought
In a concert filled with everyone, all of whom shun any form
of utterances

Gold Leaf Ashes

I observed colors, the ones we call "red", "blue," and "yellow,"
without expectation.

Who am "I" to demand, to request, to want?

The flute speaks only when the wind of God chooses to flow
through its veins
A silence however does not mean death, but rather, the
state of the first state, the permanent rest.

In time, there has come moments of that pronounced state.
Until then, this.
After that, this.

Burn effigies and salutations within wood-fired ovens
Gold leaf ashes, sprinkled liberally across the
continuous sky

The novice mystic spent the first seven years running
through the countryside collecting air with two hands.
Elevate, diminish, decrease, travel, ...
All false signs

Three songbirds, or one hundred sunflowers
Call them what you want, but I prefer you call them nothing

Sing in Silence

Rewind the rendezvous,
    Recalculate to reminisce ostentatiously
        Worried about the winding sun
Into obscurity, irrelevancy
    You picked the wrong elixir.

Assigning attributes to nothing

Find flaws is equivalent to questioning the unquestionable

Become absolutely absolute
This requires only nothing
    But a computer hard-drive reboot

Charlatans sell specific chants

There, in the tucked away mountain

Fade the ego, distill the ego, rid the ego, reimagine without
image
Light snowflakes sprinkled onto the earth's crust

Three piano keys are enough to send your soul into a frenzy

Champion emptiness,
Sing in solitude, sing in silence

Scorched Earth

Calculating mistakes is speaking a language that we were
never supposed to learn...
    Separate your eyes from the universe

A few lotus blossoms mixed with some dandelions
    A resilient bouquet that God brought to your front
lawn

Five seekers go door to door passing out bread while
children play tag in a nearby park.

Tell me who understands reality from that whose images
exist in the mind.

This life was meant just for you.

The artist creates with both hands, and the third eye.

Tigers survey their kingdom,
    Roam yours
Enter into lands distant, or blocks next door

A child presses his head against a few packed feathers
        How many generations to reach such comfort
If you see me, you are not yet there.

I existed some long time ago, when decisions made some
sort of sense, and the illusion of agency was guarded
sharply.

Now, in my back pocket, the mysteries of life.
    Or something like that.
Just make sure to burn whatever lint exists hidden in all of
the mind's corners.

Scorched Earth and scorched Mars.

Observe rows of sand and colorful umbrellas, and a crisp pre-dawn wind.

Amen is a blasphemous word...Lord accept his prayer? Who made you act the role of God?

Just watch...witness sparks and also fires quenched by overfilled skies.

Drop of My Blood

You may take every single drop of my blood
Scattering everything throughout the lands
Or leave them home, out to dry, until a hot July sun arrives.

None of this is of any difference

See how the bride combs her hair the evening before the
Wedding?
Witness the groom shine black shoes until a self-reflection is
observable

We shall enter the place of no entrance
Illustrate what cannot be captured by a sea of pirates,
What is not be held by a river filled with lily pads

A million words, a million pages
A million minutes of prayer
have destroyed any sense of separation

The blood moon is as sacred as the cloud-filled atmosphere
on that cold November night.

Burn the 99 Names

Look into the eyes of the child and see God...

     Close, a mere three steps on the long journey of holiness
     And nothingness.

Transcend awe
Transcend the mundane

Awaken by awakening, or awaken by sleeping.
Both serve the holy purpose, the meaning that is no meaning.

Note: Stop with this typing: blasphemy

Utterances are reactionary mechanisms that remove your existence from existence.

Diamond encrusted pendants are as holy as acres of grain and wild grass.

Thinking otherwise is because you think otherwise

Books indeed deserve their end fate, as does the human body
Nothing deserves what it deserves

Remove deserve, remove fate, remove "thing"

This.

The followers of Muhammad merely wondered in astonishment and recorded.
     An interrupted opinion would separate them from the halls of The Divine

Tag.

> You are it.

Children have been telling us the secrets of the universe as
early as they could talk and play games.

That is all. Anything else would be the devil's temptations
You too can make a pilgrimage to the Kaaba and throw
stones at all that exists as a growth of the mind.

> This is why God made unlimited rocks.

Use tools, and go beyond tools.

I dove head first into the waters of nothingness

> Then I cursed those who called the ocean an ocean

How dare you construct an idol of yourself?
Burn (and disconnect from) the 99 names (poems), and
enter into the 100th.

> > > Herein lies the secret for
> > > those who no longer work
> > > to understand.

Author Biography

Dr. Fait Muedini is the Frances Shera Fessler Professor, and Director of International Studies at Butler University in Indianapolis, Indiana. His poetry has been published in *Anchor Magazine*, *Allegro Poetry Magazine* and Blackmail Press. He has also published in outlets such as Foreign Affairs and Palgrave Macmillan. His most recent book is LGBTI Rights in Turkey: Sexualities and the State in the Middle East (Cambridge University Press). His poetry explores themes of Sufism, unity, beauty, and the oneness of reality.

www.ingramcontent.com/pod-product-compliance
Lightning Source LLC
Chambersburg PA
CBHW060054100426
42742CB00014B/2823